Dear Family,

What's the best way to help your child love reading?

Find good books like this one to share—and read together!

Here are some tips.

- **Take a "picture walk."** Look at all the pictures before you read. Talk about what you see.

- **Take turns.** Read to your child. Ham it up! Use different voices for different characters, and read with feeling! Then listen as your child reads to you, or explains the story in his or her own words.

- **Point out words as you read.** Help your child notice how letters and sounds go together. Point out unusual or difficult words that your child might not know. Talk about those words and what they mean.

- **Ask questions.** Stop to ask questions as you read. For example: "What do you think will happen next?" "How would you feel if that happened to you?"

- **Read every day.** Good stories are worth reading more than once! Read signs, labels, and even cereal boxes with your child. Visit the library to take out more books. And look for other JUST FOR YOU! BOOKS you and your child can share!

The Editors

For my Mommy,
who was once a girl, too
—NG

For all the girls in the circle—you know who you are!
Continue to support, encourage, and embrace one another.
With special thanks to Momma Lucille, my sisters,
and best friends E.D. and J.S.
—CAJ

Text copyright © 2004 by Nikki Giovanni.
Originally published in Quilting the Black-Eyed Pea, copyright © 2003 by Nikki Giovanni.
Illustrations copyright © 2004 by Cathy Ann Johnson.
Produced for Scholastic by COLOR-BRIDGE BOOKS, LLC, Brooklyn, NY
All rights reserved. Published by SCHOLASTIC INC.
JUST FOR YOU! is a trademark of Scholastic Inc.

Library of Congress Cataloging-in-Publication Data

Giovanni, Nikki.
  The girls in the circle / by Nikki Giovanni ; illustrated by Cathy Ann Johnson.
    p. cm.—(Just for you! Level 2)
  Originally published in Quilting the black-eyed pea, 2003.
  Summary: Three girls have fun playing dress-up at their grandmother's house, even painting their
toe nails, but then they have nowhere to go. Includes activity ideas for parents and children.
  ISBN 0-439-56861-7 (pbk.)
  [1. Clothing and dress—Fiction. 2. African Americans—Fiction.] I. Johnson, Cathy Ann,
1964- ill. II. Title. III. Just for you! Level 2.

PZ7.G43923Gi 2004
[E]—dc22
                                                                                                2004042908
10 9 8 7 6 5   08
Printed in the U.S.A. 23 • First Scholastic Printing, February 2004

The Girls
in the Circle

by Nikki Giovanni

Illustrated by Cathy Ann Johnson

The girls in the circle
have painted their toes.

They twisted their braids
with big yellow bows.

They took Grandma's face powder
and powdered each nose.

9

They sprayed Evening in Paris
all over their clothes.

They are amazed
at how they look.

They smell good, too!

Mother may not be amused.

The girls in the circle
now tease and giggle.

They look so grown up
with that high heel wiggle.

Their pearls are flapping.
Their dresses flow.

They are so sorry
they have no place to go.

Mother refuses to
drive them
anywhere
looking like that!

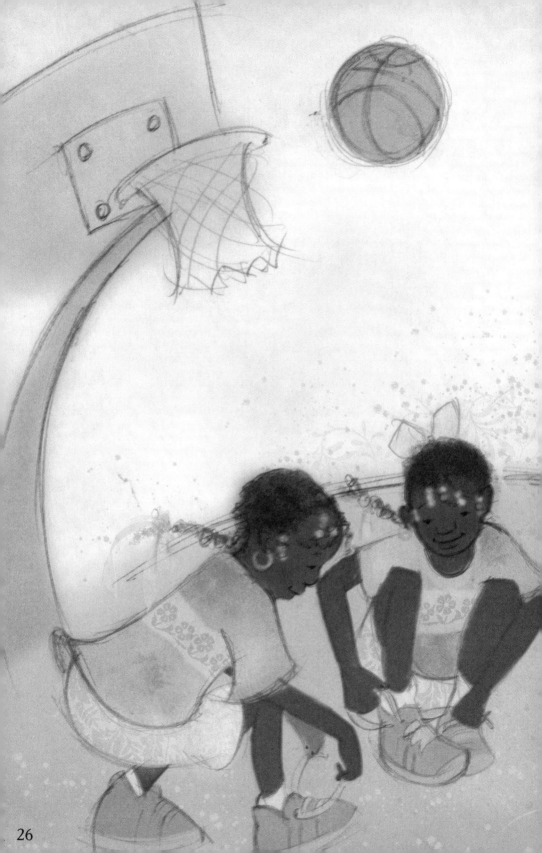

The girls in the circle
have changed their clothes.

They're tying their shoes
which are hiding those toes.

Mother thinks they took
that red polish off . . .
but they didn't!

▲▲▲▲▲▲ JUST FOR YOU ▲▲▲▲▲

Here are some fun things for you to do.

Can YOU Rhyme?

What word did the author use to rhyme with **toes**?

Nose and **clothes** also rhyme with toes.

What else rhymes with toes? ▲ Make up YOUR own rhyme!

The rhymes in this story are fun to read!

What word did the author use to rhyme with **giggle**? ▲

Jiggle and **squiggle** rhyme with giggle, too.

Can YOU make up a rhyming story with all these funny **-iggle** words? You can draw pictures to go with your story.

Read YOUR rhyme out loud!

Answers: ▲ bows ▲ wiggle

Are YOU Amused?

When people are **amused**, they think something is funny.

Do YOU think Mother was amused? Why?

Did Brother find his sisters amusing?

Tell about a time when YOU were amused.

▲▲▲▲TOGETHER TIME ▲▲▲▲

Make some time to share ideas about the story with your young reader! Here are some activities you can try. There are no right or wrong answers.

Think About It: Ask your child, "How do you know that the girls are having fun together? How do you think their brother feels about their game of dress up? How about their game of basketball?"

Play a Picture Game: This story is full of circles! Look back at the pictures. How many round objects can you and your child find? Now go on a circle hunt at home. How many circles can you find in each room?

Read More: The author of this story is a famous poet. Read aloud "About the Author" on page 32. Visit the library to find more books by Nikki Giovanni.

Act It Out: Rhymes make this story fun to read aloud, but so do the challenging words the author includes! Read the story again and point out some of these words. Talk about the meaning of *amazed* (surprised), *refuses* (says no), *flow* (move gracefully), and *giggle* (laugh). Invite your child to act out these words.

Meet the Author

NIKKI GIOVANNI says, "When I was a young girl, I used to love playing dress-up. My friends and I would put on grown-up clothes and use up Mommy's or Grandmother's perfumes. The adults would pretend to fuss at us, but they really thought we were wonderful!"

Yolanda Cornelia "Nikki" Giovanni was born in Knoxville, Tennessee, and was reared in Ohio. She graduated from Fisk University, worked with the school's Writer's Workshop, and edited the literary magazine. She attended graduate school at the University of Pennsylvania and at Columbia University in the Master of Fine Arts program. Nikki Giovanni has published numerous essays, as well as books of poetry for children and adults. She has received many awards and honors for her work, including the NAACP Image Award for Literature in 1998, 2000, and 2003, and the Langston Hughes Award for Distinguished Contributions to Arts and Letters in 1996. She is currently a University Distinguished Professor of English at Virginia Tech.

Meet the Artist

CATHY ANN JOHNSON says, "Illustrating this story brought back delightful childhood memories of the girlish, bouncy way my sisters and I used to play. I can remember the very large hallway mirror where we would spend countless giggly hours dressing up, primping, and strutting about. Oh, if only we could replay the reflections in that mirror!"

Cathy is the illustrator of several children's books, including *My Nana and Me* by Irene Smalls, and *A Heart for Jesus* by Juanita Bynum. She was born in Columbus, Ohio, and graduated from the Columbus College of Art and Design. She now lives in Kansas City, Missouri, with her son Clinton.